Beyoncé Before the Legend

The Rise of Beyoncé and Destiny's Child
The Early Years

Beyoncé
Before the Legend

The Rise of Beyoncé and Destiny's Child
The Early Years

By Kelly Kenyatta

COLOSSUS BOOKS
an imprint of Amber Communications Group, Inc.
Phoenix, Arizona

Beyoncé
Before the Legend:
The Rise of Beyoncé and Destiny's Child
The Early Years

By Kelly Kenyatta
Published by Colossus Books
an imprint of Amber Communications Group, Inc.
1334 East Chandler Boulevard, Suite 5-D67 Phoenix, AZ 85048
e-mail: AMBERBK@aol.com
www.AmberBooks.com

Tony Rose, Publisher/Editorial Director
Yvonne Rose, Associate Publisher

ALL RIGHTS RESERVED

No Part of this book may be reproduced or transmitted in any form or by any means—electronic or mechanical, including photocopying, recording or by any information storage and retrieval system without permission from authors, except for the inclusion of brief quotations in a review. Requests for permission or further information should be addressed to "The Permissions Department", Colossus Books, 1334 Fast Chandler Boulevard, Suite 5-D67, Phoenix, AZ 85048, USA.

The publication is designed to provide accurate and authoritative information in regard to the subject matter covered. It is sold with the understanding that the publisher is not engaged in rendering legal, accounting, or other professional services. If legal advice or other expert assistance is required, the services of a competent professional person should be sought.

Colossus Books are available at special discounts for bulk purchases, sales promotions, fundraising or educational purposes. For details, contact: Special Sales Department, Colossus Books, 1334 East Chandler Boulevard, Suite 5-D67, Phoenix, AZ 86048, USA.

©Copyright 2013 by Kelly Kenyatta and Amber Books
ISBN 978-1-937269-42-5

Library of Congress Cataloging-in-Publication Data

Kenyatta, Kelly.
  Beyoncé before the legend : the rise of Beyoncé and Destiny's Child : the early years / by Kelly Kenyatta.
     pages cm
  Includes bibliographical references and index.
  ISBN 978-1-937269-42-5 (alk. paper)
 1. Beyoncé, 1981- 2. Rhythm and blues musicians--United States--Biography. 3. Singers--United States--Biography. I. Title.

ML420.K675K46 2013
782.42164092--dc23
[B]

2013024276

Contents

Prelude	1
Beyoncé Knowles	3
In the Beginning	9
Destiny's Child, the First Album	13
The Writing's on the Wall	17
A New Destination?	21
Photos	25
Survivors	33
The New Destiny	39
Photos	42
On the Road with Christina Aguilera	57
Photos	61
Three Times a Charm	71
Photos	74
About the Author	77

Prelude

Beyoncé Knowles

Beyoncé's confidence in music came long before she had gained any acclaim or won any awards. The star who was born on September 4, 1981, performed in her first talent show at age seven and received a standing ovation for her rendition of "Imagine". Before the talent show ended, Beyoncé told her mother that she wanted to "get [her] trophy, get [her] money, and go, because [she was] hungry". Her mother attempted to contain her ego by explaining that the contest was over, and they did not yet know who was actually going to win the event; however, it was not long before Beyoncé's confidence was proven valid, as she was announced as the first place winner.

Years later, after achieving phenomenal international success with the group Destiny's Child, Beyoncé decided that 2003 was the perfect time in her career to release a solo album. She gained immediate acclaim, because all of her mainstream exposure had made the release of *Dangerously in Love* highly anticipated. Audiences knew that the help she received from Missy Elliot, Jay Z, Sean Paul, Mario Winans, Big Boi, and Luther Vandross would only seal the potential success of the album.

They were right. Every song that was released from *Dangerously in Love* was an instant success. The album was more passionate, more mature, and more personal than anything she had ever done with Destiny's Child. "Me, Myself, and I", "Baby Boy" and "Naughty Girl" achieved the same extreme and immediate success that "Crazy in Love" had, causing the album to reach multi-platinum status. It only made sense when she embarked on her first sold-out tour as a solo artist with co-headliners Missy Elliot and Alicia Keys.

Critics loved *Dangerously in Love* as much as her fans did. Beyoncé found herself overwhelmed as she was the biggest winner at MTV Music Awards, BET Awards, and even the Grammy Awards, where she tied the record set by Lauryn Hill in 1999 by taking home five awards.

8   *Beyoncé Before the Legend*

In the Beginning

Beyoncé began in a group called Girls Tyme in 1991 when Andretta Tillman, later Destiny's Child's co-manager and mentor, auditioned 30 girls. Six were chosen, which included all members except LeToya, who would join Beyoncé, Kelly and LaTavia over a year later.

The talented Girls Tyme, made up of 10- and 11-years-olds, attracted a lot of attention in Houston almost immediately. The fact that they were young and talented was undoubtedly the key to their success, but the girls appeared on the scene when boy groups dominated. Perhaps the time was ripe. There was Kriss Kross, Another Bad Creation, New Edition, New Kids on the Block, Hi-Five and the still popular Boyz II Men and Jodeci. As for girl groups, En Vogue was big and TLC was making its mark. Undaunted, Girls Tyme set out to have fun while making a name for itself. The songs they performed combined R&B, rap and pop with lyrics about boys and world unity. Sometimes spending six hours a day rehearsing, the girls made up most of their own dances. Their moves were forceful and imaginative, compelling their audiences to take notice. Fans who remember the kids from those days still talk about how Beyoncé, then 10 years old, pulled a little boy on stage and serenaded him, leaving him smiling and embarrassed.

The spirited Girls Tyme built up an impressive list of appearances. It included performing at a Dallas high school where they opened for the famous Yo-Yo, and performances at the Black Expo and the Miss Black Houston Metroplex pageant. The group performed at the People's Workshop's Sammy Davis Jr. Awards, hosted by recording artist Vesta. The award was bestowed on music great Bobby Womack, who performed and gave the girls early on a taste of what their talent and dedication could bring them. They were featured on a TV magazine called "Crossroads" and the group was written about in the *Houston Chronicle*, the largest newspaper in the area. It was reported that Prince called twice asking to record them on his Paisely Park record label, but that never materialized. A year after Girls Tyme formed, they made it to "Star Search," a national television show that has launched the careers of many prominent entertainers.

This was a very exciting time for the girls. They thought their singing careers were about to take off, but success narrowly eluded them. After the "Star Search" appearance, important changes happened. Three of the original six members left the group and LeToya joined the remaining three girls for the quartet that became known as Destiny's Child. That also is when Matthew Knowles, *Beyoncé's* father, became manager. He was pleased with the progress of the group so far, but he determined that changes were needed if the girls were to get to the next level. He took the group seriously enough to resign from his position as a neurological sales specialist. From that point, a group that would go on to leave its mark in the music industry was in place. Four young girls, though from different parts of Houston all attending different schools, were on their way to developing great friendships that would last for years to come. They would be spending so much time together they would become as close as sisters.

LeToya would arrive for rehearsals from Houston's south side, while LaTavia came from the northwest side and Kelly and Beyoncé from southwest Houston. Year after year, Beyoncé, Kelly, LaTavia and LeToya continued to rehearse together. They took singing and dance lessons to prepare for the great career for which they were destined. While their classmates played together after school and went to slumber parties and the mall, they missed much of that scene. They missed many a trip to AstroWorld. Instead, the girls participated in what Knowles called "Summer Camp." They kept a strict schedule where they would jog three miles each day and follow it up with eight hours of practice that included aerobics and drills.

By the time they reached high school, they had their hearts set on making it big, so they did not fall prey to the typical teenage girl distractions, like parties and boys, even if they did sing a lot about them. They knew it would all come in time. As for the time they missed on the merry-go-rounds and swings, well, they knew the world would one day become their playground. They were in part home-schooled, keeping rigorous schedules. Most of their time was spent with each other and with their families. In 1996, their schedules became so hectic their parents hired a tutor to help the girls with their schoolwork and to accommodate their schedules. It was very important to the girls and their parents that they got a good education while focusing on their music.

Cheryl Mitchell, LaTavia's mom, admitted she was concerned with how big her destined child was dreaming. She told a local reporter she did not want to discourage her daughter, but she did want to prepare her for the possibility that "her dream might not be realized." But LaTavia said that even when it seemed their careers might not work out, she never lost hope. Through good times and through the rough ones, the girls kept working toward their dreams.

Late one summer day in 1997, in a recording studio in Houston, Beyoncé, Kelly, LaTavia and LeToya were there with no recording session, publicity photo sessions or any other major engagement. The girls, dressed casually in jeans and cut-offs, chatted and giggled together. A visitor was on hand, so their manager asked them to put on a little show. Destiny's Child put on an a capella performance that stunned their guest. For the girls, it was a typical performance that came so naturally. It was the kind of performance they were used to putting on in front of church audiences since they were barely teenagers starting out together. As the visitor recalled, LaTavia's deep voice drifted in first, smooth and richer than Texas oil. Kelly and LeToya's middle-range voices sauntered in to harmonize. Beyoncé's distinctive sound streamed in and the girls harmonized. The visitor on that summer day had been a writer with a local paper. Within days, an article appeared in the paper with the writer commenting that the performance was an "aural collage so beautiful it could hardly have come from the four teenagers."

The Houston Chronicle reporter wrote:

> "*It was as if a quartet of angels had descended from the heavens. Don't be surprised if you see these Houston teens set the rhythm-and-blues industry on its ear in the next few months.*"

That's exactly what they did. The girls were already on their way.

Destiny's Child, the First Album

The year leading up to the release of Destiny's Child self-titled first album in February, 1998 was undoubtedly one of the girls' most exciting years so far. They prepared to produce the album on the Columbia record label, which meant they moved into music's major leagues. Before the album was completed, it seemed a lot of key people in the industry were taking notice of the girls and could predict their success. They were even willing to aid in it. The group was able to attract some of the most popular and talented people in R&B and hip-hop to work with them on *Destiny's Child*. Vincent Herbert, who produced hits for Brandy and Toni Braxton, handled two tracks. The Boys II Men's production team of Tim and Bob produced one track. Eleven of the tracks were produced by Dwayne Wiggins, of Tony, Toni, Tone.

Wiggins recalled first meeting the girls through a friend who signed them to a production deal when they were 10 and 11. Then in 1996, before they signed with Columbia Records, a friend played the girls' voices to him over the phone.

"I was just blown away," Wiggins told the *Houston Chronicle*. "And when they told me their ages, I was like "Yeah, right.' First of all, anyone this good would already have a deal. And no one that young would be able to blow like that."

Things heated up for Destiny's Child. The teens were overjoyed to learn they would work on their album with Wiggins at his studio in Oakland, California. In the state's Bay Area, the girls rehearsed in one of the most beautiful parts of the country. Meanwhile, there was talk of them working with Wyclef Jean and Pras, from the Refugee Camp, Master P and JD. They could hardly contain their excitement.

Week after week, they rehearsed and performed and wowed Wiggins with their talent and professionalism.

Wiggins told the *Houston Chronicle*, "I immediately knew that these girls were going to be huge. They were just like regular teenagers at times, you know, laughing and playing, which was refreshing to see. But they took their work very seriously."

The foursome worked constantly on their first album, which was mostly R&B and pop ballads with a few faster dance tracks.

Around this time, Wycleff Jean was still riveting from the mega success of The Fugee's (Refugee Camp) album, *The Score*, and his own platinum debut solo album *Wyclef Jean Presents The Carnival Featuring Refugee Allstars*. During his successful career, he had found time to work with music greats like Michael Jackson, with Sublime and Simply Red. Still, he managed to add a promising Destiny's Child to his list of artists with whom to collaborate. He dropped into Houston in July, 1997 to do a remix of the song "No, No, No" at Houston's Digital Studios. Shortly after, the video shoot for the single began. Destiny's Child also collaborated with Jean and Pras on the track "Illusion"; JD, on "With Me Part I"; and Master P, on "With Me Part II."

Evidently, Columbia was confident in the group's first album. The record company, prior to the release of the album, put "Killing Time" on the soundtrack for the blockbuster "Men in Black," starring Will Smith. The girls were flown by Columbia to New York City to do an appearance at Tower Records with Smith. They later arrived at a party at Planet Hollywood. Some of the people they had always admired were there and they mingled with them chatting and sharing laughs and congratulations. Huge celebrities there included Smith's actress wife, Jada Pinkett, Mary J. Blige and Sean "Puffy" Combs. The girls had their experience to thank for being able to handle their success and conduct themselves as young women of great maturity during the party.

Kelly told the *Houston Chronicle*, "We've done so many (shows) we can't keep track of all of them."

They had already shared the stage with double platinum SWV (Sisters With Voices), Immature and Dru Hill and had made many friends in the process. The girls gave credit to SWV for helping them learn the ins and outs of the music business.

Beyoncé told the *Houston Chronicle*, "They've been like big sisters to us. They've talked to us about pacing ourselves and watching out for people who could be hurtful to our careers."

It was good that Destiny's Child, though young, had the wisdom to listen to the accomplished artists. Their knowledge of the industry and experience greatly impressed Columbia during the deal-signing stage. The record company didn't have to worry about how the girls would conduct themselves in interviews or whether they could handle performances and fame.

When the self-titled album was released that winter, Destiny's Child was reeling from the excitement. Fans grooved to their radios and stereos and glued themselves in front of their TV sets when Destiny's Child made performances. From Houston to Jackson, Mississippi, to New York, to Oklahoma City, to Los Angeles, California, to cities and rural areas in other parts of the world, Destiny's Child set audiences on musical fire.

Beyoncé, Kelly, LaTavia and LeToya were excited about their success with the exception of one big letdown; their longtime friend and mentor Andretta Tillman passed away in 1997 from lupus. To her, they dedicated "My Time has Come." When the girls sing "And I've come much too far, and I know what's in my heart, and I know what I feel, and this time I know it's real, my time has come," they fight back the tears. They believe Tillman is looking down smiling at them, pleased that their dreams, her dreams for them, have come true. The culmination of years of hard work together started to pay off in a big way and they didn't care that it had not happened sooner. They say it simply must not have been time for them to make their big splash.

Beyoncé said in a Houston media interview, "I don't think we were ready…We wouldn't appreciate it as much if it had happened then. Now we know just how difficult this business can be."

The wait was well worth it. "No, No, No" went platinum shortly after its release and the album became the Number 1 hit on *Billboard's* Top Albums Chart. According to *SoundScan* in June, 1999, the debut album had sold nearly half a million copies. If the girls thought everything was going at a whirlwind pace before, their activity picked up at the pace of a hurricane. Tours followed and so would more in-store promotions where they met and mingled with fans and signed autographs. Destiny's Child toured the country with Boys II Men, a group they looked up to calling the members "big brothers." The girls headlined a holiday tour the following December in the UK where they performed 18 shows in 17 days. That was an amazing feat for the entertainers and the fans' response was overwhelming. They brought out the crowds in arenas in the United States and in Europe. Destiny's Child was such a hit in Europe that the girls began spending one week each month there. On both sides of the Atlantic, girls emulated their style and boys fell in love with them at first sight and first sound. And if the Destiny's Child members were tired, they never showed it. It seemed they were living on buses—they laughed about their bus actually feeling like home because they were on it so much. They kept smiling and singing their hearts out and were well received wherever they went.

To punctuate the success of Destiny's Child, the group was nominated for four coveted Soul Train Lady of Soul Awards and won in three categories. That was more nominations than were received by Janet Jackson, Erykah Badu, SWV, Mary J. Blige, Aretha Franklin or any other artist that year. The girls won for best single, best album and best new artists. The momentum continued to build.

The Writing's On The Wall

A lot of artists would have been satisfied to take it easy and rest on the laurels of their first album, but not Destiny's Child. The girls kicked their ambition up a notch and really got busy on the album that would earn them two Grammy nominations for 2000. The first album had taken them two and a half years to release. Their second tooke about two and a half months. And this time they had more creative input. Groups oftentimes don't get that opportunity, and when they do, they might not get credit for it. Being females in an industry that is run mostly by males could have presented even more of a challenge for Destiny's Child, but instead the group got its wish. The girls got to write and produce almost all of the tracks on their next album, *The Writing's On The Wall*, released in June, 1999. What a way to further heat up the summer for fans around the world! The single "Bills, Bills, Bills" was a hit all over the country and eventually was nominated for a Grammy as Best R&B song. The track also earned Destiny's Child a Grammy nomination for Best R&B Performance by a Duo or Group with Vocals. While "No, No, No" from their debut album peaked at No. 3 on the *Billboard* Hot 100, the group outdid itself when "Bills, Bills, Bills" jumped from number 11 to number 2 then moved into the No. 1 slot on the Pop Chart. Beyoncé, Kelly, LaTavia and LeToya were eating out at a restaurant in London that special day during the summer of 1999 when they found out "Bills, Bills, Bills" had jumped to the No. 1 spot. Squealing and jumping with joy, they obviously made people in the restaurant very curious about what was going on.

Women of all ages snapped their fingers and sang along with "Bills, Bills, Bills", but a lot of guys hated the song and asked why the girls couldn't pay their own bills. Destiny's Child got a good laugh out of those guys. They must be guilty of "perpin" like the triflin' fellas in the song, the girls sassily shot back. You see, they were not asking men to pay their bills. The song was misunderstood by some of the guys.

LeToya explained in an interview in *Sister 2 Sister* magazine the meaning of the hit that seemed to escape the fellas: "The song is about a relationship and the guy is treating the girl really well in the beginning, but then later on down the line he starts taking advantage of her. He's maxing out her credit cards, buying her gifts with her own money, just being irresponsible. And we're asking him to pay back the bills that he's run up and take responsibility for his actions. We ain't asking guys to just straight out pay our bills or anything like that. We aren't saying that you shouldn't help each other out in a relationship. But don't start taking advantage of each other."

As Beyoncé put it, when the guy is perpetrating with his girlfriend's car at the mall and going on shopping sprees at her expense, that couple is at the point where he pays back the bills or the two break up. The guys who had problems with that song might also have problems with some of the other sassy hits on *The Writing's On The Wall*. In "Bug A Boo", the girls sing about guys who act almost obsessed with girls, calling and paging them all the time and showing up in places they're not wanted. They also released the video that shows four girls in control of themselves, letting the guys know they are willing to socialize, but on their own terms, not because some bug a boo says "hey girl, I'm coming over right now. Be there."

"Say My Name" proved to be extremely popular number as well. It eventually became the number 1 hit in America on the *Billboard* Hot 100. Again, it was about the females saying "I'm too smart for the games you're running." The girls sang about a guy who appears to be cheating on the girl because he won't say her name during a phone conversation. She flat out tells him that someone must be there with him and if that's the case, they are so through. Similar to Christina Aguilera's top hit "I know What Girls Want," the "strong" songs were widely accepted by females who had had enough and by guys who knew the girls were telling the truth. See, for a lot of guys, the "triflin' brother" shoe didn't fit and neither did the "bug a boo" label, so instead of dissing Destiny's Child, they respected the group and snapped the albums up as quickly as they could hit the shelves of the record stores.

Beyoncé, Kelly, LaTavia and LeToya were especially proud of their latest album effort because they further showcased their multi-talents. While being pretty obviously has countless advantages, the girls realized they had to work harder for people to look beyond their physical appearances and realize they were sheer talent through and through.

"We've always wanted people to appreciate our vocals," Kelly told *Billboard*. "We don't want people to say, 'Oh, here's another pretty girl group."

"I'm excited at seeing our names in the writer and producer credits," LeToya said.

Beyoncé agreed, adding that groups are more highly regarded if members are more assertive in the creative process.

The girls recalled in an interview with *Sister 2 Sister* that the time they spent making their second album flew by because they were writing and recording on a daily basis. They wrote and co-wrote most of the songs on *The Writing's On The Wall*. Beyoncé even got to produce on most of the tracks. It was Destiny's Child's idea to include spoken commandments of relationships at the end of each song, for example, "Thou shalt pay bills," "Thou shalt not leave me wondering" and "Thou shalt not think you got it like that."

But much the same as with the debut album, the group worked with a number of key producers. They teamed up with Missy "Misdemeanor" Elliott on "Confessing" and were back with Wiggins for "Temptation". They worked with Kevin "She'kspere Briggs (who produced "No Scrubs" for TLC) on "Bills, Bills, Bills."

During the making of *The Writing's On The Wall*, Mathew Knowles, Columbia executives and the other higher ups involved with Destiny's Child decided it was time to take the girls to the top. Not only were major tours arranged, but the publicity campaign involved plans for more in-store appearances where thousands of fans came out and graciously received autographs. Internet sites were planned as was an advertising campaign promoting Soft & Beautiful Botanicals hair care products on television, radio, in magazines and on outdoor billboards. Promotional CDs containing samples of the group's music were given out in salons carrying the products. The plan to elevate Destiny's Child to the upper echelons of the music world worked.

Then at the pinnacle of the group's success, the news of Destiny's Child's break-up was announced. Naturally the February 17 announcement, just days before the Grammy ceremony, caused dismay among many of the foursome's fans. Music World Management did not say why LaTavia and LeToya left the group and neither did the departing members. The management company did report that two new members, Farrah Franklin, of Los Angeles, and Michelle Williams, of Rockford, Illinois, would join Beyoncé and Kelly. The girls already knew each other and were friends. Farrah danced in the "Bills, Bills, Bills" video. Michelle met them when she was a background singer for Monica.

A New Destination?

No, Still Stardom

Some fans believe the writing about the break-up was already on the wall. There had been some talk from callers on radio stations predicting a split was imminent. Some speculated the split would be caused by an alleged discrepancy in the girls' pay. Others claimed a rift was being caused because all of the members weren't getting a chance to showcase their talent. Some other fans who claimed to have an inside on the goings on said the departing members were leaving to pursue their education and other careers.

Regardless of what was being said by fans and insiders, Destiny's Child, management and Columbia said very little for more than a month. Media reports quoted a Columbia Records spokesperson as saying LaTavia and LeToya left the group because of creative differences.

Supposedly, it had been planned that on Grammy night, the original girls would go on stage if the group won an award. That was how fans would want it. After all, hadn't Beyoncé, Kelly, LaTavia and LeToya formed a friendship over the years that was stronger than many sisters. Importantly, the original girls had produced the hits and it was only fair they should receive the award. But the popular and longstanding TLC won in the categories where Destiny's Child had been nominated so there was little news surrounding the group at the awards. After that, the new Destiny's Child appeared together professionally. The new girls practiced more than six hours each day and appeared in the "Say My Name" video and on the Tonight Show.

Apparently the hard work paid off. The video became one of the most popular videos on television and the crowd responded positively to a fabulous performance on "The Tonight Show with Jay Leno."

Two weeks after the group restructured, the new Destiny's Child appeared on Houston's The Box radio station. Host Shelley Wade raised the topic of the break-up and asked the members to shed light on the issue and possibly dispel rumors. Wade even pointed out to Beyoncé that some people were putting the blame on her because her dad was their manager.

Beyoncé responded that such talk was upsetting. She said, "My father has done so much for everybody. As far as people saying that the reason I was lead singer was because my father was the manager, that is also totally and entirely untrue. The lead singing is based on ability. My father has nothing to do with the decisions being made on who leads the songs. That's all up to the producer. And it's up to the artist, individually, if you want to work on yourself and better yourself so you're able to lead the songs."

She added that her father never went to the producers and asked them to let her sing. She said that actually the only time he had done that was to ask whether the other girls could sing lead.

As to why her friends left Destiny's Child, she said, "It just happened like it happened. But it doesn't have anything to do with Mathew being my father. None of that."

Wade said she knew "there were a lot of legal issues going on" that the group could not talk about but offered members a chance to further address the situation if they could. Beyoncé declined saying any further talk was counterproductive.

"We're trying to work on the future and we're excited about the new girls," she said. "We're just happy because the fans are still supporting us. And the album sales are skyrocketing. We're still in the top 20 for like 28 weeks. We've been selling like 76,000 a week."

By any other public accounts, Beyoncé and Kelly wished LaTavia and LeToya well. As for the new Destiny's Child, some fans announced disappointment on Internet Web sites, letters to MTV.com and on radio stations. Others said they could accept the new girls. Regardless of what they said, fans continued to buy *The Writing's On The Wall.* Destiny's Child embarked on a European tour and on March 12, 2000 played its first live concert since Farrah and Michelle became members. The group headlined at a packed arena only days after "Say My Name" soared to No. 1 on the *Billboard* Hot 100. Beyoncé announced on stage that worldwide sales stood at 3.5 million copies.

After completing the European tour, Destiny's Child returned to the U.S. to appear with Brian McKnight at New York's Madison Square Garden. Also on the agenda were appearances on MTV, a show in Atlantic City, N.J. and at a show at Disney World in Orlando, Florida.

Although the girls were soaring in many respects, they undoubtedly were experiencing some of their roughest times as well. Farrah and Michelle were under pressure to fill LaTavia and LeToya's platforms. Beyoncé, Kelly and the two new members had to prove to fans that the new Destiny's Child was just as much a crowd pleaser as the original cast.

LaTavia and LeToya broke their silence a month after the announcement of the new members. They said it has been falsely announced they left Destiny's Child over "creative differences." In a lawsuit they filed against manager Mathew Knowles and the members of Destiny's Child, they noted they "have not withdrawn from Destiny's Child despite defendant's wrongful and malicious efforts to force them to do so." LaTavia and LeToya claimed breach of partnership duties and breach of fiduciary duties. The suit charged that Knowles and the other singers took LaTavia and LeToya's money and kicked them out of the group. The girls charged that Knowles made money from them while they themselves made virtually no money. Gerald Conley, LaTavia and LeToya's attorney, told the *Houston Chronicle* the girls earned less than $100,000, which is much less than what multi-platinum artists should earn. Conley said his clients have had no access to Destiny's Child's financial records and that it is unclear how much money was at stake.

LaTavia and LeToya charged that Mathew Knowles, Beyoncé, and Kelly "went on a rampage to destroy (their) careers." They said they were not informed about performances including the Grammy Awards and the Soul Train Music Awards. The former members named new members Farrah and Michelle as members. The new girls appear in the *Say My Name* video "even though they had nothing whatsoever to do with it," the suit charges.

Mathew Knowles responded saying he looks forward to the day when the real truth comes out. "There are and have been many creative differences," he told MTV News.

He answered one key charge saying that there had been no misappropriation of funds. He also pointed out that LeToya and LaTavia, decided to fire him, the manager of Destiny's Child without discussing it with the other members, Beyoncé and Kelly, which was "pretty insulting." Knowles said he was disappointed that at the highlight of their careers, LaTavia and LeToya "made a bad business decision."

There have been many rumors and stories, and the real story will probably never be known about why Destiny's Child split up, but the lawsuit brought an end to the speculation over why the two members actually would leave the group when it was the most successful it had ever been.

Regardless of what happened, the girls were faced with the goal of re-building their careers and undoubtedly mending friendships and wounds.

And then the world opened up and before you could "say my name" and "pay my bills," it was.

Destiny's Child before the breakup.

Destiny's Child members (l-r) Kelly, LaTavia, Beyoncé, and LeToya pose for photos after their performances at Illusion's nightclub.

Tommy Hilfiger Fashion Show: Macy's.

Destiny's Child at the Tommy Hilfiger Fashion Show at Macy's (Herald Square, NYC).

A New Destination? 27

Destiny's Child at George's Music Room in Chicago.

Destiny's Child members (l-r) LeToya, LaTavia, Kelly, and Beyoncé pose for photographers at George's Music Room after their in-store appearance.

Destiny's Child being interviewed by the "Mond Squad" at V-103 radio in Chicago.

Destiny's Child members (l-r) LaTavia, Kelly, Beyoncé, and LeToya happily pose for a photo after an on-air radio interview before the breakup.

A New Destination? 29

LeToya, LaTavia, Kelly, and Beyoncé pose pretty during happier days.

Destiny's Child greets some of their many fans.

Destiny's Child doing one of their many interviews

Beyoncé likes meeting her young fans in person.

A New Destination? 31

Beyoncé sneaks a peek at the camera while Kelendria signs autographs.

Destiny's Child backstage at The Apollo.

Survivors

February 21, the music industry's biggest night of 2001, will be forever etched in the minds of Destiny's Child and their fans. It was the 43rd Annual Grammy Awards and all eyes were on Beyoncé Knowles, Kelly Rowland and Michelle Williams from the moment they stepped out of their limousine onto the infamous Red Carpet. The music of fans screaming and saying their names played from a distance. Wearing gorgeous, cream-colored gowns designed especially for them by Versace, and dazzling smiles that were the courtesy of success, Destiny's Child was one of the night's greatest acts. The ladies had received four nominations including Record of the Year and Song of the Year for "Say My Name." Beyoncé had snagged a fifth for the songwriting of "Independent Women Part I" from the *Charlie's Angels Soundtrack*. She and Dr. Dre led the nominations.

The Grammy ritual was buzzing. Hot rapper Eminem would perform a duet with legendary Elton John. Madonna would perform the opening act. Whether performing or receiving an award, the hottest stars in the business were there including Faith Hill, Macy Gray, Jill Scott, Moby, the Blue Man Group, U2, 'N Sync, Mya, Sisqo, Christina Aguilera and hip-hop's hottest young rapper, Lil' Bow Wow. Appearing at the award ceremony were former band mates LaTavia Roberson and LeToya Luckett, who also were looking marvelous and moving forward with plans for their new group, Angel. The music that had been nominated was the music LaTavia and LeToya had written and sung with Beyoncé and Kelly so any nomination for Destiny's Child was a nomination for the four original band members. Beyoncé, Kelly and Michelle were flying high. There's no doubt about that. But the pressure was still on. There had not been a reconciliation between the former best friends so no one really knew what to expect. But the new Destiny's Child had been asked to perform so the singers put any thoughts of what could, should or would happen out of their heads. They made their way inside to change into their stage costumes and do what they do best: entertain the masses!

Dressed in sequined hot pants and matching bra tops, the beautiful, sleek and supple Beyoncé, Kelly and Michelle radiated under the spotlight. They pranced and sashayed across the stage singing strong songs: "Say My Name" and "Independent Women." The tight instrument beats rocked the house causing fans to move rhythmically in their seats. Buffed and skilled dancers swirled in the background. Beyoncé sang lead:

> *"Question: Tell me what you think about me/I buy my own diamonds and I buy my own rings/Only ring your celly when I'm feeling lonely/When it's all over please get up and leave/ Question: Tell be how you feel about this/Try to control me boy you get dismissed/ Pay my own fun, oh and I pay my own bills/ Always 50-50 in relationships."*

Their performance ended to wild applause from the Grammy audience. Shortly after, Destiny's Child was called as winner of the award for Best R&B Duo or Group with Vocal. "Say My Name" beat out "Pass You By" by Boys II Men; "9-1-1" by Wycleff Jean, featuring Mary J. Blige"; "Dance Tonight," by Lucy Pearl; and "Come Back Home," by BeBe Winans, featuring Bryant McKnight and Joe. Kelly jumped for joy backstage. Beyoncé's mouth fell open. Michelle smiled big. The ecstatic all-grown-up young women locked arms and hands and trembled with excitement as they moved toward the podium to accept their award. They held on to each as if to affirm their individual and collective existence. Would the former members come onstage, too? It would be the first time they had met in over a year. What would Destiny's Child say to the audience? Everyone's attention was on the group, just as it had been during all the chaos throughout the months.

In order to better understand how the Grammy ceremony wound up, first let's rewind the story of Destiny's Child to the beginning of 2000 and you'll see what a difference a year can really make. That was the year after LaTavia and LeToya were ousted when they attempted to replace Mathew Knowles, Beyoncé's dad, as their manager because they felt he was not acting in their best interest. Although all of the members experienced some hurt and stress from the break-up, Beyoncé was the one who spoke out about the negative personal effects the break-up had on her. She said it literally made her sick. In front of the camera and onstage she appeared to be confident and strong, ignoring those who called her bad names and playing to the fans who clamored for her. Beyoncé's mom has said her daughter's confidence goes way back to when she first performed in a school talent show when she was a 7-year-old. Tina Knowles recalled sitting among a crowd at her daughter's Catholic school watching her perform one of John Lennon's songs, "Imagine." Beyoncé did a superb job and the audience stood up to applaud her. The young girl told her mom she wanted to "get my trophy, my money and go because I'm hungry." Tina told her daughter to settle down because the contest wasn't over and that she didn't know if she would win or not. But at the end of the show, Beyoncé was indeed the first place winner.

But that confidence broke down when Destiny's Child broke up. Beyoncé said she was on the verge of a nervous breakdown. LaTavia and LeToya have said that as new adults, they felt they could choose new management for themselves, someone who would represent them fairly. Beyoncé saw things differently. She believed her ex-group mates waited until they were at their most vulnerable time— right when *The Writing's On The Wall* was taking off and the girls were preparing to do the video for "Say My Name." She told a journalist, "They felt like we would have to give them whatever they asked for. And the day they sent it (a letter terminating Mathew Knowles as manager), we were devastated. For two weeks, I literally stayed in my room and did not move. I felt like I could not breathe. I had a nervous breakdown, because I just couldn't believe it. It hurt so bad."

Being a Christian, Beyoncé said she called on her faith to help her through the rough times. Church was at the center of all the Destiny's Child members' lives since they could remember. Beyoncé, a member of Houston's St. John's Methodist Church, often went there when she was not on the road. When she lay ill in bed, she called on her memory of church fellowship, of the positive Christian energy that always embraced her. She thought back over her childhood and of how blessed Destiny's Child had been. Out of all the thousands of hard-working, aspiring artists in the world, it seemed God had chosen them. She thought back to the very beginning of Destiny's Child, when she preferred performing with LeToya, LaTavia and Kelly to playing outside. Destiny's Child was, in her opinion, some of the hungriest little girls on the planet. They practiced all the time, dreamed of success and weren't even happy unless they were onstage.

Beyoncé reflected on the times people told the little girls to make sure a career in music was what they really wanted because success would require a lot of hard work and some good fortune as well. They were right. Good times had been plentiful, but there were a number of letdowns, which she had time to think about while she suffered bouts of depression. One especially memorable episode was the time the girls sang their hearts out on "Star Search" but lost. There were times when they wanted a record deal badly, but couldn't get one. They performed showcases but left without a contract. Elektra had even signed them at one point, then dropped them. So here, many years and two hot albums later, she lay in bed wondering if it was all worth it. Remembering the ups and downs and God's gifts to her, Beyoncé began to regain her strength and confidence. If she could make it through to now, why should she retreat? Now was not the time.

She recalls climbing out of bed and fighting back. She had become hardened, so she sent her own firm letter to LaTavia and LeToya. While she had spent some of the best times of her life with them, she had also spent some of the worst times of her life with them, Beyoncé wrote. She blasted them saying they had not sung one note on some of the songs on the album, that they spent most of their time chatting on the telephone and that they lip-synched to her vocals. While the former members and some professionals they worked with deny the charges, that was how Beyoncé perceived the situation. Writing the letter was cathartic. She felt free to go out into the world and continue her work once she sent the letter on its way.

Meanwhile, Kelly's loyalty was with Beyoncé and the Knowles family, to whom she was very close. The Knowles' had shared their home with her and single mom, Doris, when they needed a more stable place to live in the early 1990's. Kelly credits her mom with being a great mother and a strong role model. In Mathew and Tina Knowles, she found a second set of parents, whom she calls Uncle and Aunt. Beyoncé and Kelly became closer.

"Beyoncé is my sister. Our relationship goes deeper than Destiny's Child," Kelly told *Ebony* magazine. "That's my sister and I love her and I know she feels the same way about me. We have each other's back, no matter what."

The break-up gave Kelly a chance to do some reflecting and soul-searching, too. She took an opportunity to look back on all she had been through as a singer. She started belting out songs in church when she was 4 years old and was captured by the music and fell in love with it, she says. She recalled the times when LeToya, LaTavia, Beyoncé and she would race home after school to watch tapes of En Vogue, who was the hottest female group around. The team of enthusiastic young girls even pretended to be En Vogue! Kelly gave up much of her childhood to achieve the level of success she gained. Like Beyoncé, she recalled the sacrifices and there would be no stopping her now, either. The two remaining members forged a tighter bond and went through what they called a "prayer week."

Beyoncé told *Ebony*, "We prayed, prayed, prayed. We said, 'God, we are not trying to put a time limit on you, but we are asking you what to do. If you send two new members to us, then that is what we will do. If not, then we know that you want Kelly and me to just finish out (promoting) the album.'"

The New Destiny

Destiny's Child needed members who could sing and dance and who also had the look, grace, style and confidence to fill the shoes of the popular members. Among the people who came to mind were Michelle Williams from Rockford, Illinois, and Farrah Franklin, from Los Angeles. Michelle was singing background for successful R&B artist, Monica. Farrah had already danced in Destiny Child's "Bills, Bills, Bills," video.

When Michelle got the telephone call inviting her to join the group, she could hardly believe it. She didn't have any illusions about show business and didn't necessarily believe success would happen overnight. Michelle had been seven when she performed "Blessed Assurance" as a solo in front of a church audience. By the time she was 12, she was directing her choir, the Martin Luther King Youth Choir made up of 500 members.

Her first big professional job was as a background singer to Monica, and granted, that was meteoric. That happened when a keyboardist friend she hadn't spoken with in several years called to chat. He had been working with Monica and Michelle expressed her interest in being a background vocalist for the singer. Her keyboardist friend called her back a week later to tell her Monica was holding auditions in Atlanta for that position. A highly ambitious Michelle flew down to Atlanta as quickly as she could. She auditioned and beat out several other girls for the job. She was living a dream life performing with Monica. She was living in Atlanta and touring with Monica and had just returned to her Rockford hometown when she heard Destiny's Child was interested in her. Michelle didn't need much time to think about whether she would accept the job because she felt that it was a great opportunity. She felt blessed, but perhaps a little in awe, a little disbelieving. She had seen others struggle much harder before getting such opportunities. At the time it was a "believe-it- when-it-happens" situation, she has said. She was prepared to keep singing background for a while. But Destiny's Child was serious about Michelle and summoned her down to Houston. The chemistry was right.

Farrah Franklin, the final component, fit the image. She was a very pretty girl and an aspiring singer who was known for her dancing, too. She had already done a superb job dancing in Destiny's Child video and had befriended Beyoncé and Kelly. At the time, the two founding members and Michelle and Farrah all said they felt very good about their relationship.

Things were happening very rapidly. They were down to the wire because Destiny's Child's schedule was packed with various performances and appearances. The new team practiced their routines for hours and hours each day. It was hard at first but they didn't intend to miss a beat. The more the new members performed together, the more comfortable they became. They immediately shot the "Say My Name" video, which became one of MTV's most popular selections. The first live performance was at an NBA All-Star weekend event that was flooded with celebrities. Shortly after they performed at the Soul Train Music Awards. The new Destiny's Child was soon on a plane headed for Europe to do their first live concert tour together. Their prayers were answered because the fans welcomed them. "It was great," Michelle recalled, "People were already screaming my name, which felt so good." She and Farrah signed autographs right alongside original members, Beyoncé and Kelly, and enjoyed their status in the hottest up-and- coming girl group on the planet. Returning to the States, they attended the 42nd Annual Grammy Awards in 2000 where Destiny's Child had been nominated for two awards but did not win.

The young ladies received word later that spring that VH1 had invited them to participate in "Divas Live," a star-studded broadcast that would be a tribute to the most renowned diva, Diana Ross. Farrah, Michelle, Kelly and Beyoncé were thrilled. They attended and performed onstage next to Ms. Ross, Mariah Carey, RuPaul, Faith

Hill and other music superstars. Although Michelle and Farrah were still new to Destiny's Child, the group's entire performance went over well. They danced on stage and promenaded through the audience singing Diana Ross's hit "Upside Down." When they finished, they were virtually in tears seeing Diana and Mariah Carey on either side of them. That was show business at its best! Diana Ross later shared with them a few words of wisdom: "Surround yourself with management you trust."

Everything appeared to be going smoothly. Offers for performances kept pouring in and Destiny's Child honored many of them. In the six months following the break-up, the singers sold more records and performed more than they had in the six months before the break-up. Some fans of the original group pointed out that the two hit albums were already in place and the new group was riding on the glory of the original band's work. Time would tell if that were true. Farrah and Michelle went into the studio to record new music with the founding members, including "Independent Women," which Beyoncé had written. She told MTV the new members were wonderful in the studio.

"It was great," she said. "The ladies, it was their first time in the studio, actually, doing 'Independent Women,' so it was a great experience for them. They did a wonderful job, and anyone that didn't know would never have known that they had never been in the studio. They were very talented."

Kelly, Beyoncé, and Michelle: The brightest stars in the galaxy, at one of their many press parties.

Destiny's Child after the breakup.

Destiny's Child and Solange after one of their hundreds of stores.

Columbia Records applauds Destiny's Child after selling 14 million albums at their "Survivor" album party.

Destiny's Child backstage at The Apollo Theater in New York City.

Kelly, Beyoncé, and Michelle with Lance Bass of 'N Sync backstage at 98.7 Kiss R&B show at Madison Square Garden, New York City, after Destiny's Child performance.

Beyoncé and Solange check out some photos from their always handy photo albums.

Beyoncé, Solange, and Tina Knowles (Mom). A family photo before the legend.

Michelle, Beyoncé, and Kelly backstage with Beyoncé's sister, Solange, at the MTV Video Awards held at the Radio City Music Hall.

Jay-Z and Beyoncé at a Roc-a-Fella Records video shoot in New York City.

Beyoncé cruises on set in a CLK Series Mercedes Benz.

Beyoncé and her sister, Solange, hang out at the Roc-a-Fella Records video shoot for Amil's song "I Got That" featuring *Beyoncé.

Destiny's Child with 3LW at the "Survivor" album release party held at The Park in New York City.

Beyoncé's sister, Solange, with 3LW at Destiny's Child album release party for "Survivor."

Beyoncé

Solange, Beyoncé's sister, backstage at Destiny's Child performance at the Fleet Center, Boston, MA. Her single "Solo Star" hit big on the "Osmosis Jones" soundtrack.

Kelly, enjoying her cake at Destiny's Child album release party for "Survivor" at The Park in New York City.

Beyoncé celebrates being a Survivor with Kelly and Michelle at their album release party for "Survivor," their third album, at The Park in New York City.

On the Road with Christina Aguilera

On any typical day, Beyoncé, Farrah, Michelle and Kelly were already up and on the move by 7 a.m. Their schedules included early morning make-up sessions, meetings with reporters, rehearsal for the night's big concert, photo shoots, radio interviews and autograph sessions with fans. But somewhere, somehow, wherever they were, they managed to get in workout sessions that included running, 500 sit-ups and 30 to 40 minutes of aerobic activity. The beautiful young women were amazingly down-to-earth and didn't for a second take their appearances for granted. They saw themselves as regular girls, so oftentimes they found time to fuss with themselves in the mirror over everything from blemishes and pimples to unruly hair to big ears to a few extra pounds.

After a typical dinner of a chicken Caesar salad at about 6 p.m., they scrubbed off their makeup and moisturized their skin, laughing and talking about the events of the day. Soon Tina Knowles would start helping them layout their outfits for the show and after that she styled their hair. The makeup artist returned to recreate their glamorous stage faces, then off to the concert they went in a luxurious limousine. Sometimes Destiny's Child would hit the stage as late as 11 p.m. Then it was back to the trailer or hotel shortly after midnight to come down from the concert and perhaps talk to a reporter or two. With a little luck, they would be in bed before 1 a.m. At least once, they went 20 straight days with the hectic schedule. Fans had no idea things weren't running as smoothly as they appeared because the young women gave it their all during the performance. But behind the scenes, Farrah wasn't happy and it would soon show.

Destiny's Child had meanwhile teamed up with one of pop music's greatest new voices. The ladies agreed to be the opening act for pretty and amazingly talented Christina Aguilera. *The Writing's On the Wall* was selling millions of copies, often out-selling Aguilera's self-titled album. Destiny's Child already had become extremely popular with young R&B and even hip-hop audiences for "No, No, No" and "Bills, Bills, Bills," but the artists were eyeing the even bigger pop audience. Teaming up with Christina allowed their popularity among the pop audience to take hold. Through the hectic pace, Destiny's Child was met with new personnel changes. With a week or so to go before the tour with Christina Aguilera was to begin, Destiny's Child announced Farrah Franklin would no longer be a member of the group and that it was the group's decision, not management's.

When asked by a fan during a FOX.com interview why Farrah left the group, Beyoncé explained: "We did 'MTV All Access' and Farrah was very tired, along with everyone else. And we had a break, talking about why Farrah was so quiet during the interview. She said she couldn't take it anymore and went home to Los Angeles. The next day we had a show in Seattle, and MTV was taping the show for All Access—it was live on the Web. Farrah didn't show up for the show. I talked to her later that day, asking her to please come to Australia with us because we had a week long promotional tour and lots of fans waiting for us. She said she didn't want to come."

When Michelle, Beyoncé and Kelly returned from Australia, they decided to continue as a trio. Farrah's story was different. She said she missed the promotional events because she was very ill and under her doctor's orders to stay back and build up her strength. She said Mathew Knowles, who had been extremely controlling and domineering, became verbally abusive with her when she told him she was sick and wouldn't be able to accompany Destiny's Child to Australia. Later she spoke out about favoritism she perceived to be shown to Beyoncé. She expressed no regrets about parting ways with her band mates of five months. She soon announced she had signed a deal with a prominent record label; she played the radiant bride in a popular R&B video and hoped to eventually act in movies.

Mathew Knowles maintains he did not deserve the flak he's taken from former Destiny's Child members but that he accepted it as part of the business, along with line-up changes.

He told Savoy magazine, "Those are things any manager goes through. I used sports as an analogy. The Chicago Bulls won six world championships. Do you know the three things they had in common for all six of those championships? Michael Jordan. Scottie Pippen. And their coach (Phil Jackson). The rest of the team changed year to year, but the core stayed the same. I kind of see Destiny's Child that way."

And he sees a long future ahead for the group, regardless of who the singers are. He points out that two of music's greatest groups, the Supremes and the Temptations, changed members many, many times. But at the end of the day, "It's all about the music," he said.

The controversy surrounding the line-up didn't appear to negatively affect record sales. Destiny's Child was in the news and *The Writing's On The Wall* kept selling. On the road with Christina, the singers were accomplishing their goal of reaching that broader audience. The tour was demanding and moved at a whirlwind pace. Reminiscent of the European tour, buses and hotels had virtually become the ladies' home again. Sometimes they went off as little as 40 minutes of sleep. They were moving so rapidly they had to pay particular attention not to get their audiences mixed up when they talked to their fans from the stage.

Their well-received tour lasted the rest of the summer of 2000 and through October. Christina entertained the audience dancing and singing her red hot "Genie in a Bottle," "So Emotional," "When You Put Your Hands on Me," and "Turn to You," among other hits. Destiny's Child pleased the crowd performing "Say My Name," "Bills, Bills, Bills," "Bug-a-Boo" and "Jump'n' Jump'n.'" Before shows, they did mall tours where they met with fans and signed autographs. City after city, the Christina Aguilera-Destiny's Child tour was the talk of the town. Christina was pleased with the opening act's performance. Calling them talented and beautiful, she also praised the performers for their ability to ad lib.

But in Denver, Destiny's Child gave new meaning to the word ad lib when Kelly had an accident backstage. She was rushing around trying to change her costume when she broke her toes. Michelle and Beyoncé kept the shows going with Kelly singing from a stool onstage. Beyoncé's younger sister, Solange, filled in doing Kelly's dance moves. Kelly announced that out of loyalty to fans, she intended to keep performing. In the end, though, Destiny's Child canceled the last shows so she could recuperate. The tour was hard work but overall it was the dream the performers had hoped for.

DESTINY'S CHILD ON TOUR

Destiny's Child on the road as the opening act for Christina Aguilera

*Destiny's Child backstage at the 42nd Annual GRAMMY Awards in 2001
Best R&B Performance By A Duo Or Group With Vocal
(wearing fashions by Tina Knowles)*

Three Times a Charm:

The Destiny's Child Trio Basks in Sweet Success

In the early fall of 2000, "Independent Women," the first song with the new Destiny's Child was being played on the radio. Beyoncé was under a lot of pressure because she had written and produced the song. She once said, "I have to prove myself every day. It's really unfair because nobody else has to do that." When she wrote "Independent Woman," she also had felt some pressure to write a song that was more positive after "Bills, Bills, Bills" had been taken the wrong way by some men who saw Destiny's Child as gold diggers. Kelly and Michelle were feeling pressure, too, after two line-up changes. Could the group still harmonize? Could they still make hits? It wasn't long before the public had its answer.

The song hit the airwaves and was immediately popular. All across the country and in other parts of the world radio stations played the song sung by the new group:

> *"The shoes on my feet/ I've bought it/ The clothes I'm wearing/ I've bought it/ The rock I'm rockin'/ 'Cause I depend on me/ If I want the watch you're wearin'/ I'll buy it/ The house I live in/ I've bought it/ The car I'm driving/ I've bought it/ I depend on me..."*

The song soon held the Billboard chart's all-time record for most airplay.

The band had lost three members and was being sued by two of them; Kelly had sustained an injury during the concert. It seems

Destiny's Child had had enough misfortune to last a while. So the rest of the year went much smoother. Kelly was getting more recognition for her vocal abilities after she recorded with popular new artist, Avant. Michelle was becoming more outgoing. They had begun working on a third album, *Survivor,* and all three members were getting bigger singing parts since Beyoncé controlled much of the producing and the songwriting. Not to be overlooked was the fact that Destiny's Child was being recognized for all the group's efforts so far. The hot female group grabbed nominations for almost every music award given including the American Music Awards, the Soul Train Music Awards, an NAACP Image Award, Block Buster Entertainment Awards, and Billboard Music Awards. Only Sisqo, who won six awards, won more Billboard Music Awards than Destiny's Child. The group won four awards and tied with 'N Sync and the Dixie Chicks to get four each. Destiny's Child won the Billboard Artist of the Year Award.

Success kept getting sweeter as they signed deals to promote Candie's footwear and AT&T. Beyoncé signed on to do L'Oreal commercials and even landed the starring role opposite Mehki Pfifer in a hip-hop television version of the movie "Carmen." During the Christmas season, LaTavia and LeToya reached an agreement with Beyoncé, Kelly and Michelle and dropped the lawsuit against them (but not against Mathew) for an undisclosed sum of money.

So by the time the Grammy Awards ceremony of 2001 rolled around, Destiny's Child was flying high. Their performance at the show was fantastic and the enthusiastic round of applause from the audience fueled the performers' strength. They got excited when their name was called out for the award for Best R&B Duo or Group with Vocal and walked out onstage with their heads held high.

"Thank you sooooo much. We are so excited. I can't believe we're winning a Grammy," Beyoncé said, beginning the acceptance speech. "First of all God, thank you so much. We want to thank all of our fans, Columbia Records, Music World Management…Oh gosh, who else?"

"All the fans," Kelly reiterated. "Thank you so much. You guys make it happen and we love you so much. God bless you."

Beyoncé continued and thanked all the writers and the producers for the album and Michelle "for blessing Destiny's Child" and Kelly. The trio happily announced their love for each other and thanked the Grammys before leaving the stage. There was no meeting up with former members who remained seated and wished Destiny's Child well. The time had not come.

What bonded Beyoncé, Kelly and Michelle as much as anything was that all members shared one common goal: for Destiny's Child to be the #1 group in the world— not just in R&B, but all categories. For 2001, it can be argued that that is exactly what Destiny's Child was. And the members keep developing their already exceptional talents.

Beyoncé told MTV, "I think it is important to look good and to dance, but I think it's more important to be a true artist than a half-talent because beauty fades. There are millions of beautiful people in the world. There have been millions of beautiful bands that have come and gone. If you don't have any substance and talent behind it, then after one or two albums there's another beautiful band there to take your place."

She added, "When I perform, that's the happiest point I can be at in life… There is nothing that compares to that joy, especially when you look to your right and to your left and you see these ladies. It is beautiful, and sometimes when we do all our thank-yous to each other, we get all teary-eyed and cry and just catch the Holy Spirit because it feels so good. We feel with God's help, nothing can hold us back."

Once upon a time, there were four little girls from Houston, Texas…

Beyoncé performs with Jay-Z

Beyoncé and Cuba Gooding, Jr. strike a pose

Beyoncé and Jay-Z share a proud moment on the Red Carpet

About the Author

Kelly Kenyatta is a Chicago-based writer and freelance journalist. She has written for major newspapers and magazines and holds bachelor's and master's degrees in journalism.

Photo Credits:
Walik Goshorn
Raymond Boyd
Mark Scott

ORDER FORM

WWW.AMBERBOOKS.COM

Fax Orders: 480-283-0991 / Telephone Orders: 602-743-7211
Postal Orders: Send Checks & Money Orders Payable to:
  Amber Books
  1334 E. Chandler Blvd., Suite 5-D67, Phoenix, AZ 85048
Online Orders: E-mail: Amberbk@aol.com

____ *Beyoncé Before the Legend,* ISBN #: 978-1-937269-42-5, $12.00
____ *Kanye West Before the Legend,* ISBN #: 978-1-937269-40-1, $15.00
____ *Nicki Minaj: The Woman Who Stole the World,* ISBN #: 978-1-937269-30-2, $12.00
____ *Eminem & The Detroit Rap Scene,* ISBN#: 978-1-937269-26-5, $15.00
____ *Too Young to Die, Too Old to Live: The Amy Winehouse Story,* ISBN#: 978-1-937269-28-9, $15.00
____ *Lady Gaga: Born to Be Free,* ISBN#: 978-1-937269-24-1, $15.00
____ *Lil Wayne: An Unauthorized Biography,* ISBN#: 978-0-9824922-3-9, $15.00
____ *Black Eyed Peas: Unauthorized Biography,* ISBN#: 978-0-9790976-4-5, $16.95
____ *Red Hot Chili Peppers: In the Studio,* ISBN #: 978-0-9790976-5-2, $16.95
____ *Dr. Dre In the Studio,* ISBN#: 0-9767735-5-4, $16.95
____ *Tupac Shakur—(2Pac) In The Studio,* ISBN#: 0-9767735-0-3, $16.95
____ *Jay-Z…and the Roc-A-Fella Dynasty,* ISBN#: 0-9749779-1-8, $16.95
____ *Ready to Die: Notorious B.I.G.,* ISBN#: 0-9749779-3-4, $16.95
____ *Suge Knight: The Rise, Fall, and Rise of Death Row Records,* ISBN#: 0-9702224-7-5, $21.95
____ *50 Cent: No Holds Barred,* ISBN#: 0-9767735-2-X, $16.95
____ *Aaliyah—An R&B Princess in Words and Pictures,* ISBN#: 0-9702224-3-2, $10.95
____ *You Forgot About Dre: Dr. Dre & Eminem,* ISBN#: 0-9702224-9-1, $10.95
____ *Michael Jackson: The King of Pop,* ISBN#: 0-9749779-0-X, $29.95

Name:_____
Company Name:_____
Address:_____
City:_____ State:_____ Zip:_____
Telephone: (____) _____ E-mail:_____

For Bulk Rates Call: **480-460-1660**   **ORDER NOW**

Beyoncé	$12.00
Kanye West	$15.00
Eminem	$15.00
The Amy Winehouse Story	$15.00
Lady Gaga	$15.00
Nicki Minaj	$12.00
Lil Wayne: An Unauthorized Biography	$15.00
Black Eyed Peas	$16.95
Red Hot Chili Peppers	$16.95
Dr. Dre in the Studio	$16.95
Tupac Shakur	$16.95
Jay-Z…	$16.95
Ready to Die: Notorious B.I.G.	$16.95
Suge Knight:	$21.95
50 Cent: No Holds Barred,	$16.95
Aaliyah—An R&B Princess	$10.95
Dr. Dre & Eminem	$10.95
Michael Jackson: The King of Pop	$29.95

❏ Check ❏ Money Order ❏ Cashiers Check
❏ Credit Card: ❏ MC ❏ Visa ❏ Amex ❏ Discover

CC#_____
Expiration Date:_____

Payable to:
  Amber Books
  1334 E. Chandler Blvd., Suite 5-D67
  Phoenix, AZ 85048

Shipping: $5.00 per book. Allow 7 days for delivery.

Total enclosed: $_____

www.ingramcontent.com/pod-product-compliance
Lightning Source LLC
Chambersburg PA
CBHW071735040426
42446CB00012B/2368